FIERCE
CREATURES

FIERCE
CREATURES

Steve Parker

Miles Kelly
PUBLISHING

First published in 2003 by
Miles Kelly Publishing Ltd
Bardfield Centre,
Great Bardfield,
Essex, CM7 4SL

Some material in this book first appeared in
10 Things you should know about

2 4 6 8 10 9 7 5 3 1

Editorial Director: Anne Marshall
Project Editor: Belinda Gallagher
Assistant Editor: Lisa Clayden
Design: HERRING BONE DESIGN

ISBN 1-84236-301-8

Printed in Hong Kong

British Library Cataloguing-in-Publication Data

A catalogue record for this book is available from
the British Library

www.mileskelly.net
info@mileskelly.net

Contents

Sharks

Dinosaurs

Spiders

Crocodiles

Big Cats

1 Sharks love meat!

Shark facts
- Great whites grow to over 7 metres in length.
- Great whites live in warm seas and oceans around the world.
- Great whites are rare as so many have been killed by people.

Sharks hunt the meat or flesh of other animals. The **GREAT WHITE** is the biggest, fiercest hunting shark of all. It feeds on almost any prey, from small fish to great whales – and even people. The great white is also called a 'man-eater'.

The great white's teeth are up to eight centimetres – as long as a finger. And there are more than 50 of them!

8

Great whites are so dangerous, divers who study and photograph them stay in a strong safety-cage.

Jumbo shark!

The biggest great white ever weighed was 4 1/2 tonnes. That's as heavy as a full-grown elephant!

The great white is certainly great, but it's not white – it has a dark grey back, and a pale grey or cream underside, often with dark scars from old wounds.

2 Sharks cannot chew!

Shark facts
• The whale shark grows to more than 15 metres long.
• Whale sharks can weigh over 20 tonnes.

Most sharks are big. The **WHALE SHARK** is a giant! It is the world's biggest fish, but is not a fierce hunter. It swims with its mouth open, filtering small animals such as fish and krill from the water with its special comblike gills. Like all sharks, it cannot chew — it just swallows its food whole!

The whale shark has only very small teeth in its huge mouth.

Whale sharks often lie still just under the surface of the water. Are they sunbathing or resting? No one really knows for sure.

Tiny snacks

The whale shark's food includes small fish, and shrimplike animals called krill – each about as big as your little finger.

The whale shark has a spotty back and pale underside.

Big sharks often have smaller fish, like these pilot fish, swimming with them.

Sharks have super senses!

Shark facts

- The great hammerhead is more than 5 metres long.
- Sometimes hammerheads have dozens of stingray stings stuck in their throats.

Sharks like the **HAMMERHEAD** are super-sensitive. They can smell blood in the water from five kilometres away. In clear seas they can see for 30 metres ahead of them. They even sense tiny amounts of natural electricity in the water, made by their prey.

Water-wings!

The 'hammer' is like an underwater wing. It helps the shark to swim well and stay up near the surface.

The snout (nose area) detects tiny bursts of electricity in the water which are made by other animals as they move.

The eye and nostril are at the very end of the amazing lobed head.

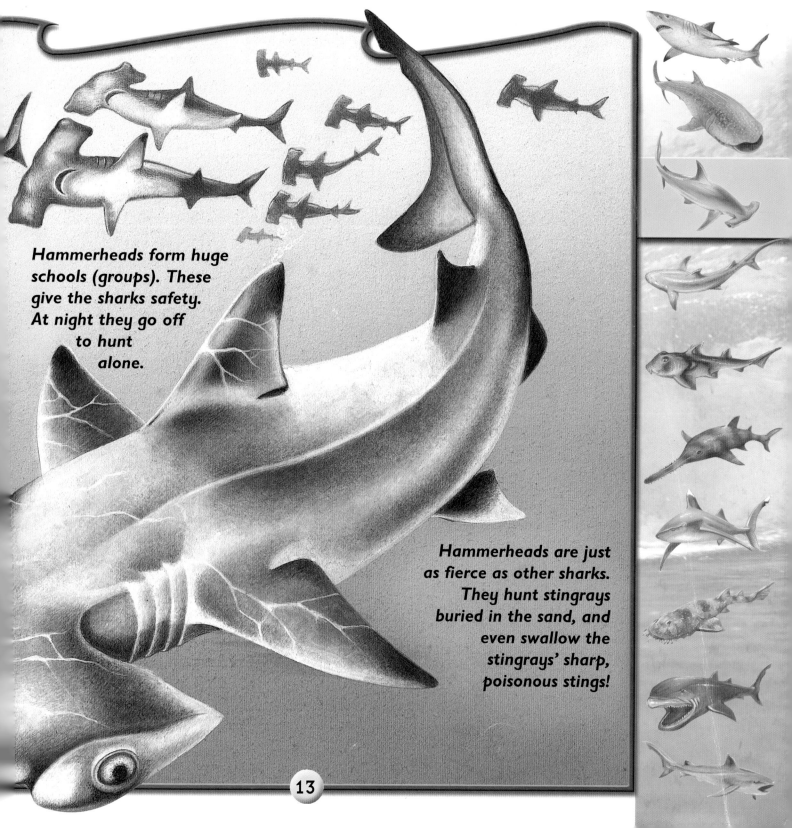

Hammerheads form huge schools (groups). These give the sharks safety. At night they go off to hunt alone.

Hammerheads are just as fierce as other sharks. They hunt stingrays buried in the sand, and even swallow the stingrays' sharp, poisonous stings!

4 A deadly tail!

Sharks swish their tails to and fro, to swim fast. But the **THRESHER** uses its tail in another way too – as a weapon! It flicks its long tail about like an underwater whip, bashing small fish to wound or stun them. Then the thresher snaps them up in its mouth.

Shark facts
- The thresher's tail can be 3 metres – half the shark's total length.
- Threshers are also called fox sharks or swingle-tails.

The thresher's teeth are small and triangle-shaped, but they're very sharp, just like short knife blades.

Threshers eat small fish like herring, mackerel and pilchard, which live in huge shoals. The sharks swim through the shoal, thrashing their tails. This stuns the fish, allowing the threshers to swim back and eat them.

A baby is born!

A few mother sharks, like the thresher, give birth to babies rather than laying eggs. The baby is 160 centimetres long.

In a shark's tail, the upper part, or lobe, is longer than the lower one. In the thresher's case — it's a lot longer! (In other fish the two lobes are about equal.)

5

Eggs and babies

Some sharks lay eggs, like the mother **PORT JACKSON SHARK**. She sticks them to rocks or weeds on the seabed. A few weeks later the baby sharks hatch out. They're hardly bigger than your hand. They look just like their parents — and start to hunt straight away!

Each back fin has a sharp, pointed spine just in front of it — to act as protection against other sharks.

The eggs are attached to rocks or pebbles on the seabed.

Port Jacksons are in the group called horned or bullhead sharks. They have a horn-like ridge above each eye, and a wide, blunt head. They can lie still on the seabed for hours.

Screwy egg!

Port Jackson eggs are up to 20 centimetres long. A strange screw-shaped ridge holds the eggs among the rocks.

Small, sharp front teeth in the down pointing mouth grab shellfish, crabs, shrimps and worms. Bigger, flat rear teeth crush them.

6 Sharks are very scaly!

6

Shark facts
- The saw shark reaches about 1.2 metres in length.
- Saw sharks are related to saw fish and both have a long, saw-shaped snout.

A shark's skin is covered by small scales. These are very sharp and pointed – in fact, they are just like tiny teeth. The **SAW SHARK** also has teeth outside of its mouth. These run in a row along each side of its long snout. The saw shark 'saws' into mud and seaweed to find fish and starfish, and eats them using the teeth in its mouth.

The snout teeth look like a chainsaw and are just as dangerous.

On each side of the snout is a long, bendy feeler – a barbel. It wriggles like a finger in the mud to find food.

Be a saw shark!

You can make any kind of shark mask, from stiff card. But the saw shark looks one of the fiercest and funniest!

The saw shark has a flattened body which is ideal for lying low! It spends most of its time swimming or resting on the seabed.

7 Sharks like to sleep!

Shark facts
- White-tipped reef sharks are 2 metres in length.
- They hunt fish, crabs, lobsters and even octopuses.

Sharks don't just swim and hunt. Some like to have a rest. **WHITE-TIPPED REEF SHARKS** sleep by day in caves or under rocks. They often rub their backs against the rocks to get rid of pests. But at night, they go their separate ways and swim off to hunt.

The white-tipped fins make this shark easy to recognize.

These sharks may be still by day, but if a tasty fish comes near – they wake up in a flash!

This big fin, on the side of the body near the front, is a shark's pectoral fin.

Close eyes!

When a shark attacks, a special piece of skin called a membrane slides down to protect its eyes.

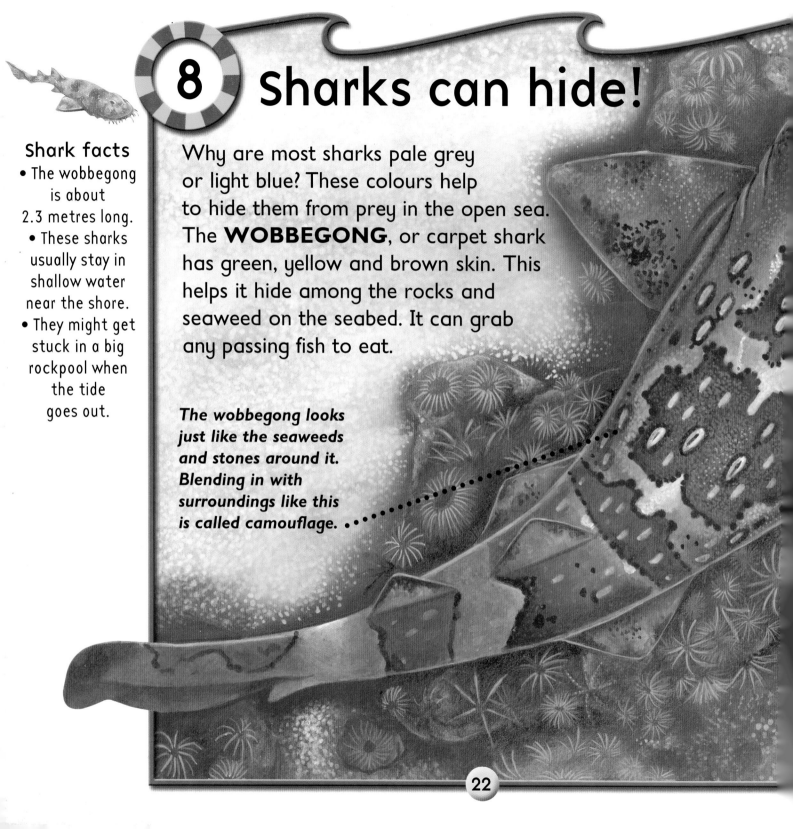

8 Sharks can hide!

Shark facts

- The wobbegong is about 2.3 metres long.
- These sharks usually stay in shallow water near the shore.
- They might get stuck in a big rockpool when the tide goes out.

Why are most sharks pale grey or light blue? These colours help to hide them from prey in the open sea. The **WOBBEGONG**, or carpet shark has green, yellow and brown skin. This helps it hide among the rocks and seaweed on the seabed. It can grab any passing fish to eat.

The wobbegong looks just like the seaweeds and stones around it. Blending in with surroundings like this is called camouflage.

Carpet shark!

Find a carpet with plenty of colours. Get some patches of paper the same colours. Sticky-tape them onto some old clothes and lie on the carpet. Are you well camouflaged, like the wobbegong?

The wobbegong lies very still on the seabed waiting for a meal. It may not move for hours!

9 A bendy skeleton

Shark facts
- The megamouth is 4.5 metres long.
- It weighs about 1 tonne.
- Megamouths live in deep water where it is very dark.

The **MEGAMOUTH** is a mysterious shark of the deep ocean. Like other sharks, it has no bones! Every shark has a strong skeleton inside its body, with parts like a skull and ribs. But these parts are not made of bone. They are made of rubbery, bendy material called cartilage.

New discovery!
No one had ever seen a megamouth until 1976, when one was caught near Hawaii in the Pacific Ocean.

The megamouth does not chase after prey, like most other sharks. It swims along slowly.

The megamouth's mouth really is mega! It's about one metre across – and it glows in the dark! But the teeth are tiny.

Like whale sharks and basking sharks, megamouths suck in tiny animals such as krill and baby fish.

The loose skin and floppy fins show that the megamouth is a slow swimmer.

10 Deadly sharks!

Shark facts

Shark facts
- Tiger sharks reach more than 6 metres in length.
- They are wide and bulky too, so they can weigh more than 1.5 tonnes.
- Some people who were thought to be eaten by great whites, were probably attacked by tiger sharks.

Some sharks have huge appetites and will eat almost anything. The **TIGER SHARK** eats fish, seals, turtles, dolphins, sea birds, squid, crabs, other sharks, and almost anything else. Tiger sharks have also been known to swim along the coast and attack people in water that's only waist-deep.

In a shark, new teeth are always growing to replace the ones which wear out or snap off. So the tiger shark is always ready to bite!

The tiger shark is big and powerful. It could swallow this monk seal in one gulp.

Tiger sharks are born with stripes on their sides. These fade as the shark gets older.

Dustbin shark!

Tiger sharks have swallowed leftover food thrown from ships, also tin cans, lumps of wood, training shoes, and even a tom-tom – a type of drum!

Tiger sharks can be big and heavy. Some can even rival great whites in size.

11 King of the dinosaurs

TYRANNOSAURUS REX was one of the biggest hunting animals ever to walk the Earth. This massive meat-eater had more than 50 teeth — each one of them was bigger than your hand.

Dinosaur facts

- Tyrannosaurus was 12 metres in length.
- It lived in North America.
- It was one of the last dinosaurs and lived about 65 million years ago.

Dinosaur name

- Say it: 'Ty-ran-owe-saw-rus-rex'.

- It means 'king of the tyrant lizards'.

Tyrannosaurus weighed about 7 tonnes — that's as heavy as two elephants.

The teeth of *Tyrannosaurus* had wavy, saw-like edges called serrations. They could easily slice through the flesh of its victim.

Even bigger!

Giganotosaurus was another meat-eating dinosaur. It was even larger than *Tyrannosaurus*!

The arms of **Tyrannosaurus** were tiny and probably useless.

12 Hammer-tailed dinosaur!

Dinosaur facts
- Ankylosaurus lived 70 million years ago in North America.
- It was 10 metres long and weighed 5 tonnes.

Dinosaur name
- Say it: 'An-kill-owe-saw-rus'.
- It means 'stiff or fused lizard'.

ANKYLOSAURUS had two heavy lumps of bone at the end of its tail. It could swing these at enemies like a huge hammer. But for most of the time, this dinosaur was a peaceful plant-eater.

Ankylosaurus was protected by long spikes of bone on its head • • • • • • • • • • • • • • • *and shoulders.*

Each lump of bone on the tail was as big as a basketball.

Bony tail

The tail club of *Ankylosaurus* was made of bone, which had become stuck, or fused, together.

Pieces of bone as big as dinner plates, and very hard scales, protected the back of Ankylosaurus.

Ankylosaurus crouched down to protect its soft underside.

Hunting in packs

Dinosaur facts

- Deinonychus was 1.6 metres high – as tall as a human.
- It lived in North America 110 million years ago.

Dinosaur name

- Say it: 'Day-non-ee-cuss'.
- It means 'terrible claw'.

DEINONYCHUS went on the prowl in a group or pack. In this way it could attack prey much bigger than itself, like a one-tonne *Tenontosaurus*. This gave enough food for a whole week!

Some dinosaurs died and their bones, teeth and claws were preserved as fossils. The fossils of several Deinonychus were found together, showing that they lived and hunted in groups.

Deinonychus *had strong back legs. It could run fast, jump high and leap a long way.*

Clever dinosaur?

The brain of Deinonychus was quite big compared to other dinosaurs. It may have been pretty clever!

Deinonychus *slashed out with its powerful hand claws.*

The toe of Deinonychus had a huge, curved claw. This was used to rip open its victim.

Plate-backed dinosaur

Dinosaur facts

- Stegosaurus lived about 150 million years ago in North America.
- Stegosaurus was 9 metres long and weighed 2 tonnes.

Dinosaur name

- Say it: Steg-owe-sore-uss'.
- It means 'roof lizard'.

STEGOSAURUS had tall, thin plates of bone on its back. Why? Perhaps they soaked up the Sun's heat, to make this dinosaur warm. The hotter *Stegosaurus* got, the faster it moved.

Stegosaurus *had a mouth shaped like a bird's beak, for pecking at plant food.*

The back plates were
as tall and wide as
a pillow. But they
were only as thick
as your wrist.

Tiny brain

Stegosaurus was as big as an
elephant, but its brain was as
small as your thumb. So it
wasn't very clever!

Caring mother

Dinosaur facts

• Maiasaura was 9 metres in length.
• It lived 80 million years ago in North America.

Dinosaur name

• Say it: 'My-ah-sore-ah'.
• It means 'good mother lizard'.

The big plant-eating dinosaur **MAIASAURA** laid its eggs in a bowl-shaped nest, which it scooped in the soil. It protected the eggs from hungry enemies and even fed the babies when they hatched.

*Fossils have been found of **Maiasaura** nests, babies and grown-ups. The nests were quite close together, in a group called a breeding colony.*

*The **Maiasaura** nest was about two metres across and contained around 20 eggs.*

*Each baby **Maiasaura** hatched from an egg about as big as your two fists placed end-to-end. Its leg bones were not quite strong enough for it to run around.*

The mother Maiasaura brought leaves and berries back to the nest, for her babies to eat.

Mega eggs!

Some mother dinosaurs laid eggs 30 centimetres long – the size of a rugby ball – and as big as 50 hen's eggs.

Speedy dinosaurs

Fast-running dinosaurs like **ORNITHOMIMUS** were called 'ostrich-dinosaurs'. This is because they were very similar in size and shape to the bird of today, the ostrich. Perhaps they ran as fast, too!

Dinosaur facts

• Ornithomimus was about 3 metres long and lived 75 million years ago.

Dinosaur name

• Say it: 'Or-nith-owe-mim-uss'.

• It means 'like an ostrich'.

Ornithomimus *had powerful muscles in its hips and upper legs, to take long, quick strides.*

The lower legs and feet were long, slim and light.

The long neck of Ornithomimus helped it to peck on the ground.

Ornithomimus had no teeth at all! Its long, beak-shaped mouth was suited to pecking and snapping up all kinds of foods, from leaves to little lizards.

Fastest!

An ostrich-dinosaur or an ostrich would not quite catch the fastest runner today – the cheetah.

Ornithomimus had a top speed of 80 kilometres per hour – twice as fast as a champion human sprinter.

Noisy dinosaurs

Dinosaur facts

- Parasauro-lophus lived 70 million years ago in North America.
- It was 10 metres from nose to tail.

Dinosaur name

- Say it: 'Pa-ra-sore-owe-loaf-uss'.
- It means 'beside ridged lizard'.

The plant-eater **PARASAUROLOPHUS** had a long tube of bone sticking up from the back of its head. This was hollow. Perhaps the dinosaur blew air through it to make loud noises – just like an elephant does when it 'trumpets' through its trunk.

Perhaps Parasaurolophus *made noises to frighten off enemies. These noises may have helped to attract a mate, or warned other herd members of danger.*

Dino-song!

Roll a card sheet into a long tube. Shout and make noises through it. Maybe that's how dinosaurs 'sang'!

Parasaurolophus breathed air in through its nose. The air passed up and down inside the hollow tube, before it went into the body.

The bony tube had no hole at the end. Its tip was sealed.

18 Dinosaur giant!

Dinosaur facts

- Brachiosaurus was 25 metres in length.
- It lived 140 million years ago in Africa, Europe, and North America.

Dinosaur name

- Say it: 'Brack-ee-owe-sore-uss'.
- It means 'arm lizard'.

BRACHIOSAURUS was one of the biggest dinosaurs that ever lived. It weighed over 50 tonnes — more than a huge juggernaut truck. It was also one of the tallest dinosaurs. Its head could stretch to 13 metres above the ground.

Giant feet!

Brachiosaurus had huge feet and made footprints one metre across — bigger than a school desk.

Because of its huge size, Brachiosaurus *must* have spent its whole life eating. Its neck was more than 8 metres long, the same length as a flag pole!

Brachiosaurus *had a* small head and peglike teeth for pulling leaves off twigs.

The front legs, or 'arms', were longer than the back legs, adding to the great height of Brachiosaurus.

The smallest of all

Dinosaur facts
• Compsognathus lived 150 million years ago in Europe.

Dinosaur name
• Say it: 'Comp-sog-nay-thuss'.
• It means 'elegant jaw'.

COMPSOGNATHUS was just about the tiniest dinosaur. However, even though it was small, it was very fierce. *Compsognathus* was a speedy hunter of little creatures such as insects, worms – and perhaps baby dinosaurs.

Compsognathus *was small and slender. It weighed only three kilograms – less than an average pet cat.*

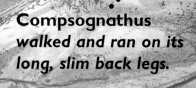

Compsognathus *walked and ran on its long, slim back legs.*

The head on the long, bendy neck could dart about and snap up prey.

Compsognathus had many small, sharp, curved teeth for biting its tiny victims.

The arms of Compsognathus had sharp claws for grabbing food.

Micro dino!

Compsognathus was about as tall as a chicken of today, but much thinner – and without the feathers.

Dinosaur horns and frills

Dinosaur facts

• Triceratops lived 65 million years ago.
• It was 9 metres long and weighed 5 tonnes.

Dinosaur name

• Say it 'Try-sarah-tops'.
• It means 'three horns on the face'.

TRICERATOPS was usually a quiet, peaceful plant-eater. But if an enemy came near, it charged with its head down, and jabbed with its long, sharp horns. The wide frill of bone over its neck made it look even more fearsome!

Like all dinosaurs, Triceratops had tough, scaly skin.

Triceratops *had to defend itself against the great meat-eater Tyrannosaurus. These two dinosaurs lived at the same time in the same region.*

Shadow dino!

Put your fingers in the positions shown, between a desk lamp and the wall. See the shadowy dinosaur!

The nose horn of Triceratops *was quite short. But the horns over the eyes were more than 1 metre long.*

47

21 Fierce spiders

Spider facts
• The Sydney funnelweb lives in Eastern Australia.
• Its head and body are 4 to 5 centimetres long.
• It can live for more than five years.

Some spiders are very shy. If you go too near, they hide in a dark corner. The **FUNNELWEB SPIDER** of Australia may do this – or it may rear up, show its big fangs, and get ready to strike.
This is very dangerous.
The funnelweb is a big, strong spider, and its bite can kill a person.

Prey get trapped by the outer silk threads and the spider poisons them with its bite.

48

..The funnelweb feeds at night on insects trapped by its silk threads. It feels for its food in the dark with its long front legs.

Spider danger!
Where poisonous spiders live, never put your hands into holes or corners. Use a stick to lift rocks or plants. Wear gloves and boots.

The threads make a funnel shape that leads to the spider's lair – a hole under a rock or root.

22 Wonderful webs

All spiders can make silk threads, but not all spiders make webs from them. The **ORB-WEB SPIDER** weaves a beautiful web shaped like a wheel. It has strong, straight threads, which look like the spokes on a wheel, and sticky spiral threads to catch the spider's prey.

Spider facts
• Orb-web spiders live all over the world, especially in woods and hedges.
• They are usually 1 to 3 centimetres in length.

New from old!
The orb-web spider makes a new web each day. First, it eats the old one, to recycle it. This means less new silk has to be made.

Long, straight threads give the web strength.

Spiral threads are soft, stretchy and sticky. Flies and moths just can't escape from them.

The whole web takes about one hour to build.

If the spider has just eaten, it will wrap up any new prey in silk threads, and store it at the web's edge. This is a snack for later on!

The spider waits in the middle of the web. When a victim gets caught and struggles, the spider feels the threads pull with its feet. It follows the tugs to find its meal.

51

23 Spiders can swim!

Spider facts
- The water spider lives in ponds, lakes and ditches in Europe and parts of Asia.
- Its head and body are 1.5 centimetres in length.

Few spiders live in water. In fact, there's only one! The **WATER SPIDER** breathes air like other spiders. By bringing small air bubbles under the water, this spider uses them to make a bigger bubble. This bubble home provides the spider with air.

The big bubble or 'air bell' is the water spider's home. It stays inside most of the time. It eats, rests, and even breeds there.

The spider spins a dome of silk threads tied to water plants and pebbles. These trap the big bubble of air.

The spider visits the surface to gather air. It traps small air bubbles between its legs and in its body hairs. It carries them underwater to add to the big bubble.

The spider pokes its legs out of the bubble to see if it can catch tadpoles, insects and tiny fish. It dashes out to bite them, and brings them back to eat.

Sea spider

The sea spider looks like a spider and lives in the sea. But it is not a real spider, just a close cousin.

Spider facts

- Black widows live in warm parts of the world.
- They are found in many habitats, from grasslands to gardens.
- The head and body are 1.3 centimetres in length.

All spiders have a poisonous bite, to kill prey or stop it struggling. But only a few spiders have poison powerful enough to harm a person. One which does is the **BLACK WIDOW**. It is small, shiny and black, and its bite can kill a human. So can its close cousin, the redback spider.

New for old!

All spiders grow by casting off, or moulting, their 'skin' — the old body case. There's a new, bigger one underneath.

The female black widow is usually the one which harms people. If she feels threatened, she tries to hide or run away. But sometimes she has to bite in self defence.

After mating the female may eat the male! This is why she is called the black 'widow'. She no longer has a partner.

The female black widow is larger than the male. She has a red mark shaped like an '8' on the underside of her body.

25 Big, hairy spiders

Spider facts

• Big, hairy tarantulas and bird-eating spiders live in tropical places.

• The head and body are up to 12 centimetres in length.

• The legs measure more than 25 centimetres across.

The biggest spiders in the world are hairy and huge – bigger than your hand. These **TARANTULAS** or bird-eating spiders really do eat birds, especially baby birds in nests. They also hunt insects, worms, and even lizards, mice and baby rats!

This female tarantula is guarding her eggs. They are surrounded by a shell, or cocoon, of silk. When the babies hatch, they look like tiny versions of their mother.

As dusk falls, the tarantula sets off to hunt. Most types prowl around on the ground, but some actually live in trees.

Spider hands!

Put on an old pair of gloves and stick two buttons to the thumbs. Link your thumbs together and walk like a tarantula!

Tarantulas have huge fangs which can bite very hard. But most are not especially poisonous. They rely on their strength and size.

26 Some spiders spit!

SPITTING SPIDERS don't spit ordinary spit. They squirt a sticky liquid, like glue, from their fangs. This sprays over their prey like a rope or net. The prey gets tangled up and stuck down. Then the spitting spider moves in, delivers its poison bite, and begins to feed.

The spitting spider has only six eyes, not eight like other spiders.

Spider facts

- Spitting spiders grow to 1.2 centimetres.
- They live in all regions except Australia and New Zealand.

58

Spitting spiders catch tiny insects such as ants, flies, gnats and midges.

The spit becomes thick and sticky as soon as it comes out of the spider's fangs.

Spitting spiders often hunt on fences and walls around houses.

The spider shakes its head from side to side as it sprays. So the spit forms two wavy, zig-zag ropes that fall onto the victim and pin it down.

Spitting distance

The spitting spider can spit three times its own length!

Spider facts
• Raft spiders live in marshes, swamps and ponds around the world.
• Most are large, with a head and body up to 4 centimetres long.

The **RAFT SPIDER** sits on a leaf or stone, at the edge of a pond or marsh. Its front legs dip in the water and detect the tiny ripples of small creatures moving nearby. The spider dashes across the water, grabs its victim, and races back to land to eat its meal.

Raft spiders are big enough to grab young fish, water insects, pond snails, tadpoles and even small frogs.

The raft spider feels for its prey with its front legs and also with its palps – these look like short legs on either side of the fangs.

The spider's hairy body, legs and feet trap tiny bubbles of air. These stop the spider sinking under the water's surface.

Fishing for flies!

Fish for flies using a magnet, string and paper clips with paper 'wings'. The 'flies' stick to the magnet if you're quick enough!

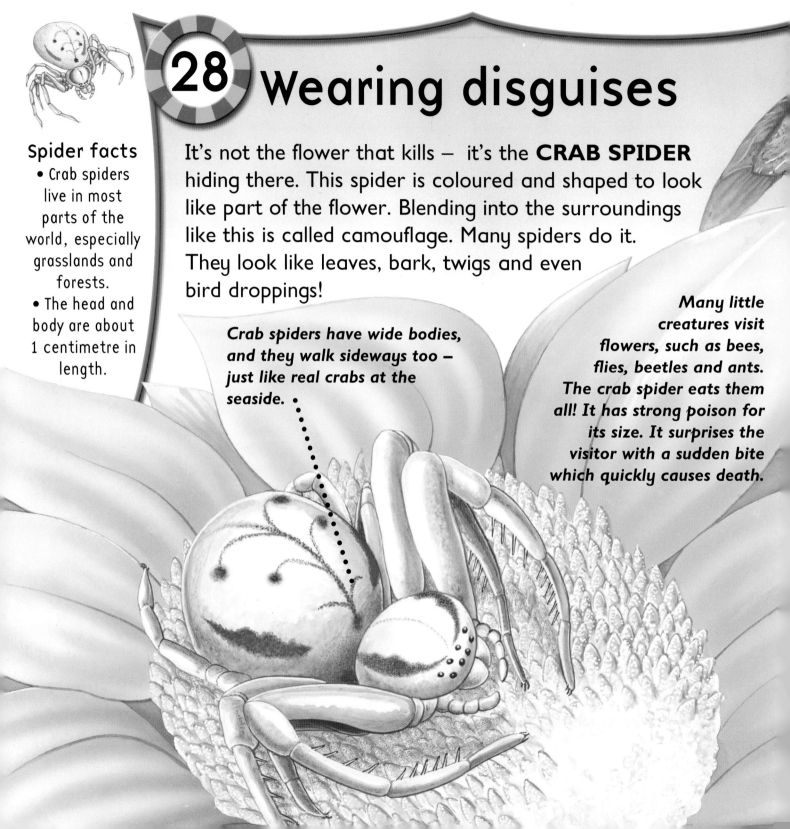

28 Wearing disguises

It's not the flower that kills — it's the **CRAB SPIDER** hiding there. This spider is coloured and shaped to look like part of the flower. Blending into the surroundings like this is called camouflage. Many spiders do it. They look like leaves, bark, twigs and even bird droppings!

Spider facts

• Crab spiders live in most parts of the world, especially grasslands and forests.

• The head and body are about 1 centimetre in length.

Crab spiders have wide bodies, and they walk sideways too — just like real crabs at the seaside.

Many little creatures visit flowers, such as bees, flies, beetles and ants. The crab spider eats them all! It has strong poison for its size. It surprises the visitor with a sudden bite which quickly causes death.

Crabs of many colours!

Crab spiders come in many colours, from white, yellow and pink, to red, green and grey. They always sit in a flower of the same colour.

The crab spider keeps very still, until the victim is close enough to bite.

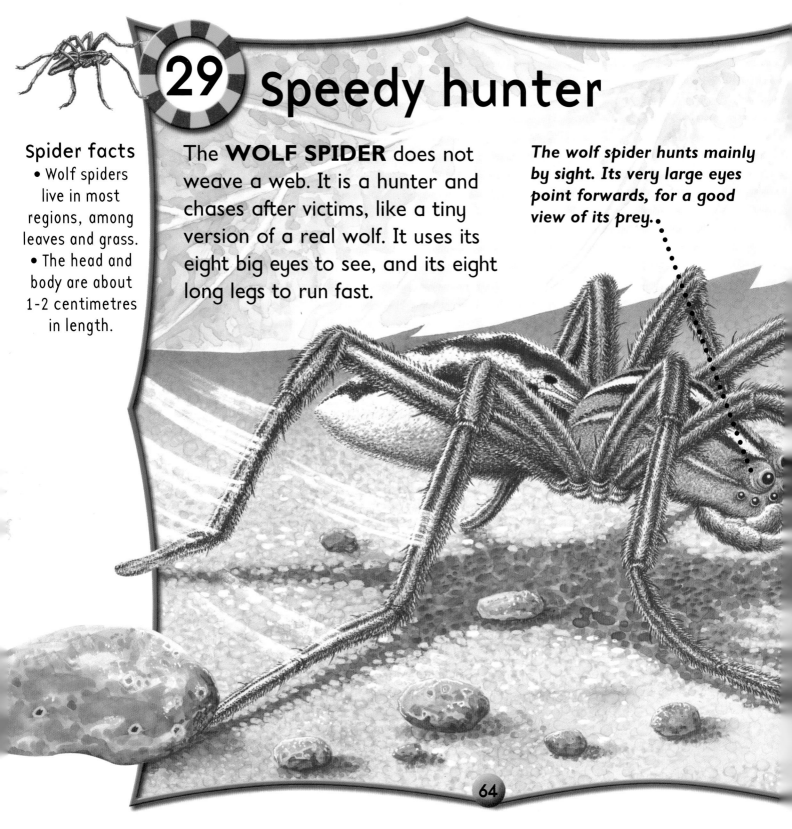

29 Speedy hunter

Spider facts
- Wolf spiders live in most regions, among leaves and grass.
- The head and body are about 1-2 centimetres in length.

The **WOLF SPIDER** does not weave a web. It is a hunter and chases after victims, like a tiny version of a real wolf. It uses its eight big eyes to see, and its eight long legs to run fast.

The wolf spider hunts mainly by sight. Its very large eyes point forwards, for a good view of its prey.

All spiders have a large head, with eight legs attached, and a rounded body. The wolf spider's head and body are small, but its legs are very long and strong.

Wolf spiders sunbathe on pebbles, soil or leaves before they hunt.

The wolf spider eats any creature it can catch, from a slow slug to a leaping cricket.

Making babies!

The female wolf spider lays eggs and wraps them all in a silk case for protection. A few weeks later, the baby spiders hatch.

30 Spiders hate baths!

Spider facts
- House spiders live in outbuildings, homes and sheds.
- The head and body are up to 2 centimetres in length.

HOUSE SPIDERS don't go in the bath to get clean. They prowl about at night, go too near the edge of a bath or sink, and slide in by accident. They can't climb back out because the walls are too steep and slippery. They need help!

The palps feel the way.

The fangs seize and bite prey.

Save a spider!

Put a glass over the spider, slide card under it and lift the card and glass together. Put the spider outside. If you can't do this – ask someone who can!

House spiders are helpful. They eat flies, mosquitoes and other pests. If there's one in the bath or sink – save it!

House spiders spin untidy-looking webs in corners. The sheetlike web is triangle-shaped. It's called a cobweb.

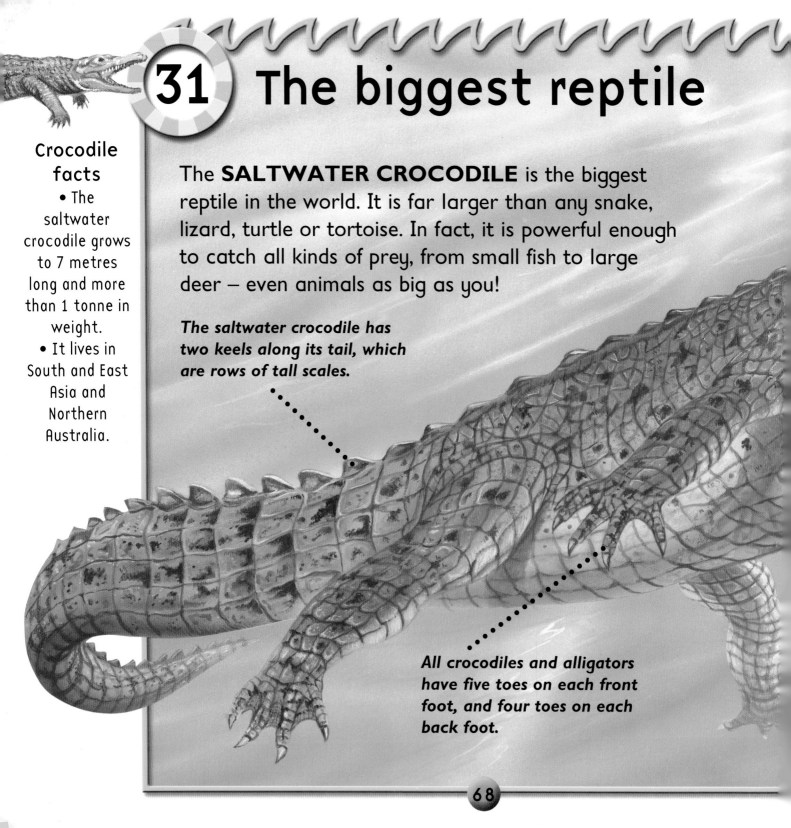

Crocodile facts

- The saltwater crocodile grows to 7 metres long and more than 1 tonne in weight.
- It lives in South and East Asia and Northern Australia.

The **SALTWATER CROCODILE** is the biggest reptile in the world. It is far larger than any snake, lizard, turtle or tortoise. In fact, it is powerful enough to catch all kinds of prey, from small fish to large deer – even animals as big as you!

The saltwater crocodile has two keels along its tail, which are rows of tall scales.

All crocodiles and alligators have five toes on each front foot, and four toes on each back foot.

Saltwater crocodiles live in swamps, rivers and lakes. They are fierce and dangerous, especially if they are surprised or cornered. They are true 'man-eaters' and have killed many people over the years.

Seaside croc!

The saltwater crocodile gets its name because it lives in rivers and lakes, but it can also swim out to sea. Other crocodiles and alligators hate salty water!

Muggers steal fish!

Crocodile facts
• The mugger grows up to 4 metres in length.
• It lives in the Indian region.

The **MUGGER** is a strong, powerful crocodile that likes any kind of fresh water. It even hides in man-made ditches and canals. In big lakes, it follows fishing boats and then steals the fish from the nets! The mugger's jaws and teeth are strong enough to crush a turtle's shell, or drag a water buffalo under the surface so that it drowns.

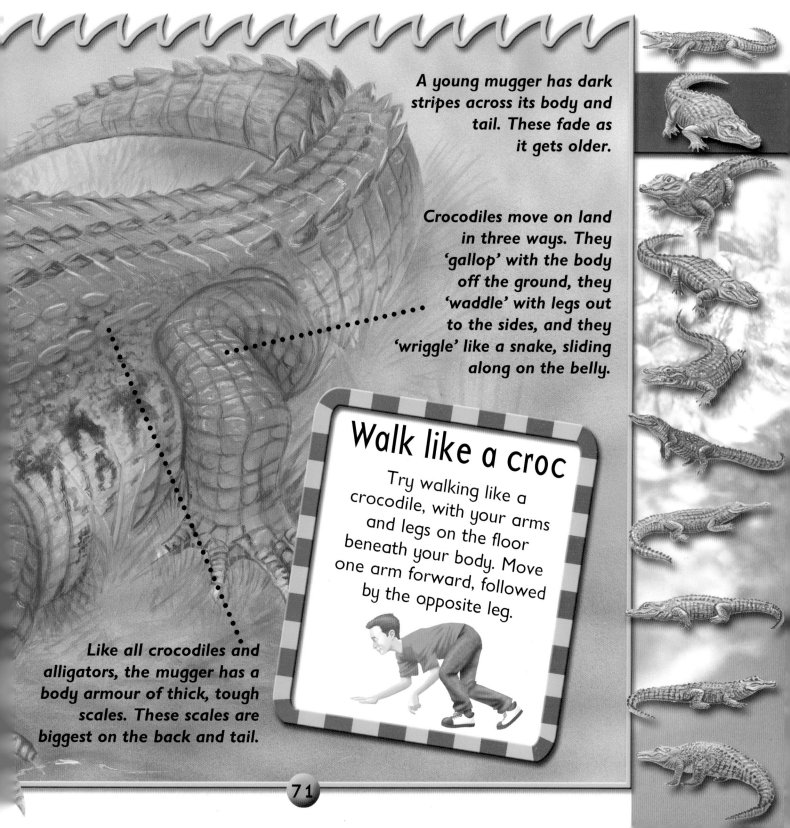

A young mugger has dark stripes across its body and tail. These fade as it gets older.

Crocodiles move on land in three ways. They 'gallop' with the body off the ground, they 'waddle' with legs out to the sides, and they 'wriggle' like a snake, sliding along on the belly.

Walk like a croc

Try walking like a crocodile, with your arms and legs on the floor beneath your body. Move one arm forward, followed by the opposite leg.

Like all crocodiles and alligators, the mugger has a body armour of thick, tough scales. These scales are biggest on the back and tail.

Some crocodiles are small

The **DWARF CROCODILE** is one of the smallest crocodiles. It is so little, that one frog is a big feast! So is a fish, a crayfish or a baby water bird. Unlike most crocodiles, the dwarf crocodile does not like to sit in the sun. It hides among plants by day and comes out to hunt at night.

Swish that tail!

Hold your hand on its edge in water, and swish it to and fro. This is how a crocodile uses its tail to swim. A flat hand has less power.

The dwarf crocodile may be small, but it is very well protected. It has lots of thick scales all over its body – even on its eyelids.

The dwarf crocodile is also called the short-snouted crocodile, because its nose and jaws are not very long.

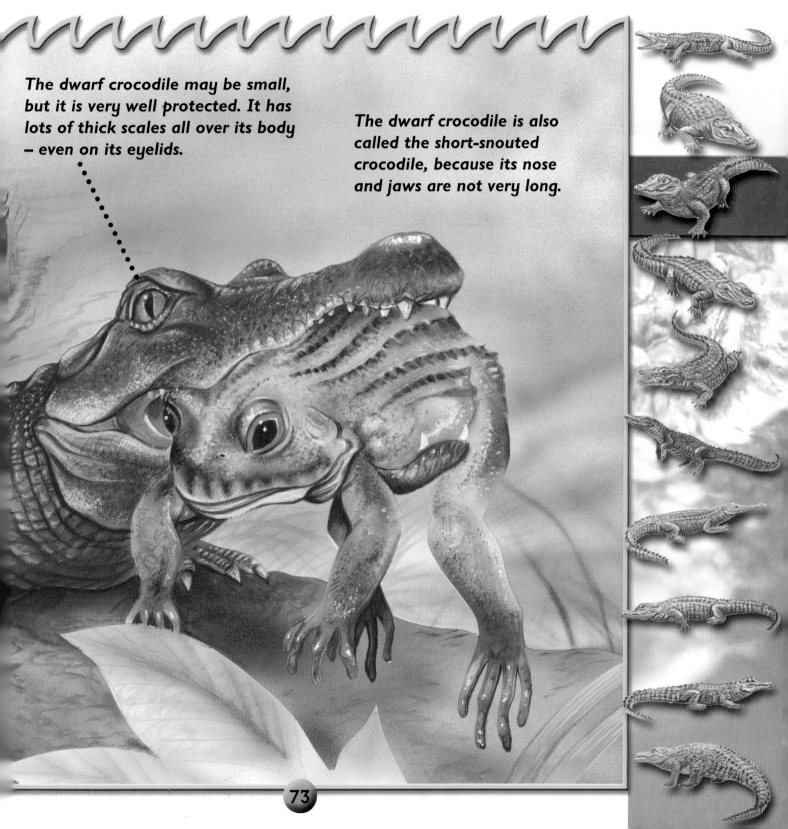

34 Alligators are good mothers!

Alligator facts

- The American alligator grows to about 5 metres long.
- It lives in North America in swamps, rivers and lakes.

The female **AMERICAN ALLIGATOR** is a caring mother. She makes a huge pile of mud and plants, lays her 40 to 50 eggs inside, and guards them well. When the babies are ready to hatch, they squeak inside their egg shells. Their mother carefully digs them out.

The female alligator carefully pulls each egg from the nest so that the baby can break out of its egg shell.

The nest mound is like a compost heap. As the plants rot, they make heat that keeps the eggs warm.

The baby alligator inside the egg is about 22 centimetres long. After it hatches, its first meal will probably be a water insect or baby fish.

Caring mums!

With nearly all crocodiles and alligators, the female is a caring mother. She guards her eggs and babies fiercely.

35 Crocodiles always have new teeth!

Caiman facts

- The black caiman may grow to 6 metres long.
- It lives in rivers and swamps in the Amazon region of South America.

Like other crocodiles and alligators, the **BLACK CAIMAN** grows a new tooth almost every week. The old teeth get worn, chipped and broken, and fall out one by one. Each time, a new tooth grows from inside the jaw to replace the lost one. A crocodile is never toothless!

Caimans are a type of alligator. There are five different kinds of caiman and they live only in Central and South America.

Dino-crocs!

Crocodiles were around before the dinosaurs, over 200 million years ago. Some were a gigantic 15 metres long!

Black caimans are not all black. They have patterns of white spots, and grey and yellow patches, on a brown or black background.

The black caiman is the biggest hunting animal in South America. It eats large fish, turtles, water snakes, deer, and pig-like animals called tapirs. It even eats smaller kinds of caimans.

36

Crocodiles like to lie in wait!

- The American crocodile sometimes grows longer than 6 metres.
- It lives in southern North America to northern South America.

The **AMERICAN CROCODILE** spends most of its time doing nothing. It lies on the riverbank or floats in the water. This is part of its clever hunting method. Animals wander past, stop to drink, and SNAP! They get dragged into the water and torn to pieces!

As a crocodile floats in water, perfectly still, it looks like a harmless old log. Its eyes and ears are above the surface, as is its nose, so that it can breathe. The crocodile looks and listens, waiting for its next meal.

Crocodiles are cold-blooded, like other reptiles such as snakes and lizards. If the weather is cool, they can only move very slowly. After they warm up their bodies by lying in the sun, they can run as fast as you!

Longer = older!

Crocodiles live to a great age – if they stay out of trouble. The older they are, the longer they grow. Some are over 100 years of age!

American crocodiles sometimes gather in groups. They come together where there is lots of food. The feast might be a shoal of fish, or a group of pig-like animals called peccaries, which have drowned in a flood.

37

Hunting underwater

• The gharial (gavial) grows to more than 6 metres long.

• It lives in northern parts of the Indian region.

The **GHARIAL** breathes air into its lungs, like other crocodiles. But it can hold its breath and stay underwater for a long time — more than half an hour. Gharials can also hunt underwater, and even eat their prey there.

Gharials spend a lot of time in the water, chasing fish. They do not move about on land as much as other crocodiles.

Like all crocodiles, the gharial has flaps of skin called webs, between its toes. These help to push through the water when swimming.

To swim fast, crocodiles swish their tails and steer with their feet. They can also swim slowly by just paddling with their feet.

Bumpy nose!

The male gharial has a lump on the front of its nose, at the tip. The female gharial does not.

The gharial's long snout is very thin. It has lots of small, pointed teeth – perfect for catching slippery fish.

Alligator facts

- The Chinese alligator is one of the smallest of the crocodile group – less than 2 metres long.
- It lives in only a few areas of China.

Crocodiles do not rush about. They are still for much of the time, as they soak up the sun and watch for prey. If the weather is cold crocodiles have to lie still, because they are too cool to move. The **CHINESE ALLIGATOR** is still all winter. It sleeps in a cave or burrow and wakes up in the warmth of spring.

Rarest of all!

Chinese alligators are rare. They live in only a few areas of the lower reaches in the Chang-Jiang (Yangtze) River.

The Chinese alligator lives mainly in this pink shaded area

CHINA

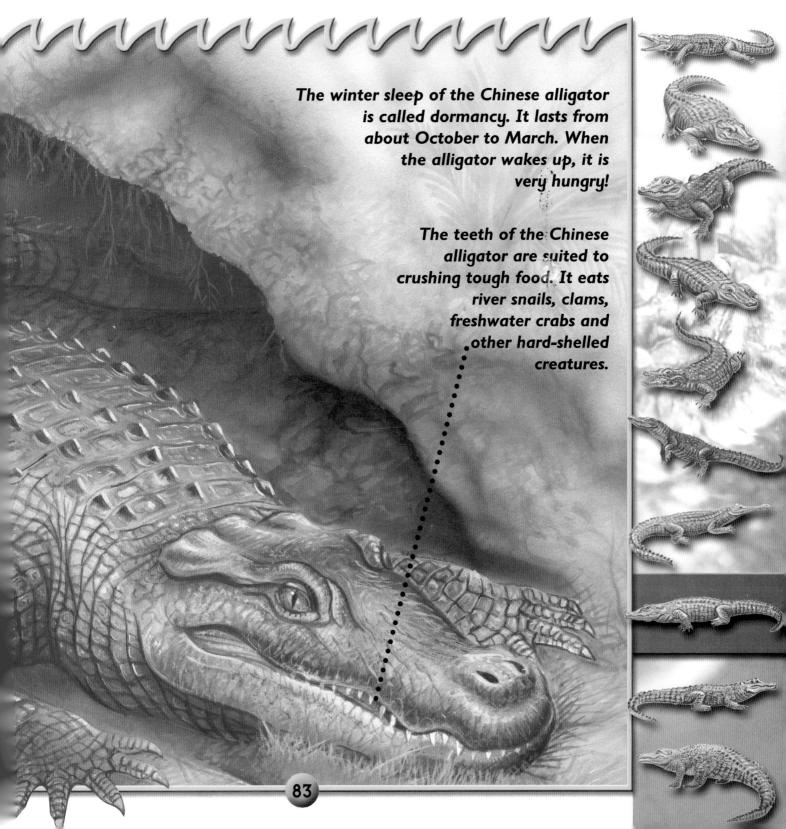

The winter sleep of the Chinese alligator is called dormancy. It lasts from about October to March. When the alligator wakes up, it is very hungry!

The teeth of the Chinese alligator are suited to crushing tough food. It eats river snails, clams, freshwater crabs and other hard-shelled creatures.

39 Crocodiles are not fussy

Caiman facts

• The common caiman lives in many parts of Central and South America.

• It rarely grows longer than 3 metres.

The **COMMON CAIMAN** likes any fresh water, from natural lakes and rivers, to man-made canals, ditches, and the reservoirs which collect behind dams. It even lies in the water troughs put out for farm animals. When they come for a drink — SNAP!

The common caiman has a bony ridge in front of each eye. It looks as if it is wearing glasses. This is why sometimes it is called the spectacled caiman.

Caimans catch fish, water birds and river snails. They even eat piranhas – fierce fish with sharp teeth.

The common caiman has the strongest body armour of almost any crocodile. Each piece is as thick and tough as the heel of a boot.

On the move

Common caimans prefer swampy areas, but will move around to live almost anywhere. They have even been known to survive in dry grasslands.

40 Crocodile killers!

Crocodile facts

- The Nile crocodile can reach almost 6 metres in length.
- It lives in many parts of Africa.

There are 23 kinds of crocodiles, alligators and caimans. One of the most dangerous is the **NILE CROCODILE**. Each year it kills more people in Africa than lions do! Luckily, after a big meal, a crocodile can last for a month or two before it's hungry again.

The Nile crocodile waits in the muddy water, for a thirsty animal to come and drink.

When a crocodile relaxes with its mouth wide open, birds such as spur-winged plovers pick its teeth clean – and get their own meal.

Many crocodiles swallow stones, to make themselves heavier. Then they can float unseen, just below the surface, right up to their prey.

Croc farms

Well-fed crocodiles living on farms grow almost twice as fast as those in the wild.

41

Tigers are biggest

Cat facts

- The Siberian tiger measures 3.5 metres long, from nose to tail-tip.
- It weighs up to 300 kilograms – as much as five adult people.

The **SIBERIAN TIGER** is not just a big cat – it's the biggest cat! This huge hunter prowls the cold, snowy lands of Eastern Asia. It is the rarest kind of tiger, too, with less than 200 left in the wild. The Bengal tiger of the Indian region is more common, with about 5000 living wild.

The tiger has long fur on its cheeks, making its face look wide.

The Siberian tiger has thick fur to keep it warm in the ice and snow of winter.

Tigers have black stripes on their yellow, orange or gold fur. The Siberian tiger has more white in its coat to help it blend in with its snowy landscape.

Man-eaters!

Very rarely, tigers attack and eat people. These tigers are usually old or injured. They can't catch their normal prey such as deer, wild cattle and wild pigs.

The Siberian tiger is heavily built. Its body hangs close to the ground.

42 Pumas make good mothers

Cat facts
• The puma has a nose-to-tail length of 2.2 metres.
• It lives in western North America and South America.

Like all big cats, the female **PUMA** is a very caring mother. She protects her babies, feeds them on her milk – and keeps them warm and safe in a den.

Baby big cats are called cubs. Puma cubs have spotty coats when they are first born. These fade as they get older.

Puma cubs feed on their mother's milk for about seven weeks. Then they begin to eat pieces of meat which their mother brings back to the den.

The mother cat licks her babies clean. She often moves them to a new den for extra safety.

Useful tails

Like the puma, the domestic cat has a long tail. This helps it to balance as it walks along narrow surfaces, and as it runs.

A mother puma usually has two or three cubs, but there may be as many as six!

43

Lions live in groups

Cat facts
• The male lion is 3 metres long and weighs 200 kilograms.
• The female lion is 2.5 metres long and weighs 130 kilograms.

LIONS are the only kind of cat that live together in a group. All other cats live alone (except for a mother with her babies). A group of lions is called a pride. There are usually between five and ten lions in a pride. They are mostly mothers with their young, and one or two males. Most lions live in Africa, with just a few hundred in India.

In a pride, the chief male lion is the father of all the cubs. His main job is to chase away other lions, so that they cannot steal prey from the pride's area.

The lion is the only big cat where the female and male look different. The male is bigger and has long, shaggy neck fur called a mane.

Padded paws

Lions have thick, leathery pads on the underside of their paws. These help the lion to move quietly and get a good grip on slippery rocks.

Male and female lions roar loudly. This frightens off other lions which aren't in their pride.

44

Jaguars love water

Cat facts

• The jaguar grows up to 2.5 metres long, including its tail.

• It is a heavily built cat and weighs up to 150 kilograms.

• Jaguars live in Central and South America.

Many cats hate water and getting wet. The **JAGUAR** loves it! This big cat is sturdy and strong, with large, powerful muscles. It likes to hunt around rivers, lakes and swamps, and it can swim well. The jaguar catches water creatures such as turtles, caimans (types of crocodiles), crayfish and snakes. It even dives under the surface to chase fish!

After a swim, the jaguar cleans and combs its fur, using its rough tongue and its sharp claws.

American cat!

The jaguar is America's biggest cat. With its spotty coat, it is similar to the leopard of Africa and Asia.

Each 'spot' on the jaguar's coat is like a ring with a dark centre. The patchy pattern helps the jaguar to blend in with leaves and twigs.

The jaguar creeps slowly through water without a splash or a ripple. It surprises prey such as deer and tapirs.

45 Caracals can leap

Cat facts

- The caracal is about 1 metre long, including its tail.
- It lives in Africa and the Middle East.

All cats can jump well. But one of the best leapers, for its body size, is the **CARACAL**. It is not a very big cat, yet it can spring forwards more than 4 metres in one bound. It can even jump 3 metres in one leap – straight upwards!

The caracal is also called the desert lynx, because it likes dry areas – and because its ears have long tufts of fur like a real lynx.

The caracal eats rats, hares, birds, and baby animals such as antelopes and wild pigs. It also eats lizards and snakes.

The caracal lives in dry places such as rocky hills, grassland, scrub, and around the edges of deserts. Its gold colour makes it difficult to spot among the brown plants and sandy soil.

Champion leap!

The caracal can jump four times its own body length. See how far you can jump – as if you are practising for the long jump!

The caracal crouches down and then springs forwards using its powerful rear legs.

46 The lynx likes snow

Cat facts
• The lynx is about 1.2 metres long, including its short tail.
• Various kinds of lynx live in the north of Europe, Asia and North America.

The **LYNX** is at home in the snow and ice of the far north. It has very thick fur to keep it warm. Even the tips of its ears have furry tufts. Its paws are large and wide, and they have fur underneath, too. The paws work like snowshoes, to prevent the lynx sinking into soft snow, or sliding on slippery ice.

The lynx has a very short tail, less than 20 centimetres in length. A long tail might get so cold in the freezing winter, that it could suffer from frostbite.

Like many cats, the lynx searches for prey which are old, young, sick, or injured. These are easier to catch than strong, healthy prey!

Snow-paws!

Press your fingers into flour, which is soft and white, like snow. Now put a bag over your hand. See how your 'snow-paw' sinks in less.

The lynx hunts deer, wild sheep and goats, hares and birds. It may bury spare food in the snow and come back to eat it later.

The lynx's paws are wide and furry. They give a good grip on snow, ice, wet rocks and slippery tree branches.

47 Snow leopards have sharp claws

Cat facts
• The snow leopard lives in the high mountains of central Asia.
• It measures 2 metres long from nose to tail-tip.

The **SNOW LEOPARD**, like other big cats, has five toes on each front foot and four toes on each back foot. Every toe has a sharp claw! The claws grip trees and rocks when climbing, and they slash and slice prey when hunting.

The snow leopard also uses its claws to comb its fur and scratch its skin.

The rare and beautiful snow leopard hunts in mountain forests and crags. It catches wild goats, sheep, birds, monkeys and squirrels.

Smallest cat

The smallest kind of big cat is the clouded leopard of Southeast Asia. It lives almost all of its life in trees.

Like other cats, the snow leopard usually keeps its claws retracted. This means they are pulled back inside its pads, which are like pockets at the ends of its toes. This keeps the claws clean and sharp.

48 Servals have super-senses!

Cat facts
• The serval is about 1.2 metres long, but it is very slim and weighs only 15 kilograms.
• It lives around lakes and rivers in Africa.

All cats have amazing senses to help them hunt at night. The large eyes of the **SERVAL** see well in the dark. Its long, stiff whiskers help it to feel its way. The serval's big ears pick up sounds and its nose sniffs for food and danger. The serval is unusual for a cat as it also hunts by day.

The serval has spots on its body, but stripes on its neck and upper legs.

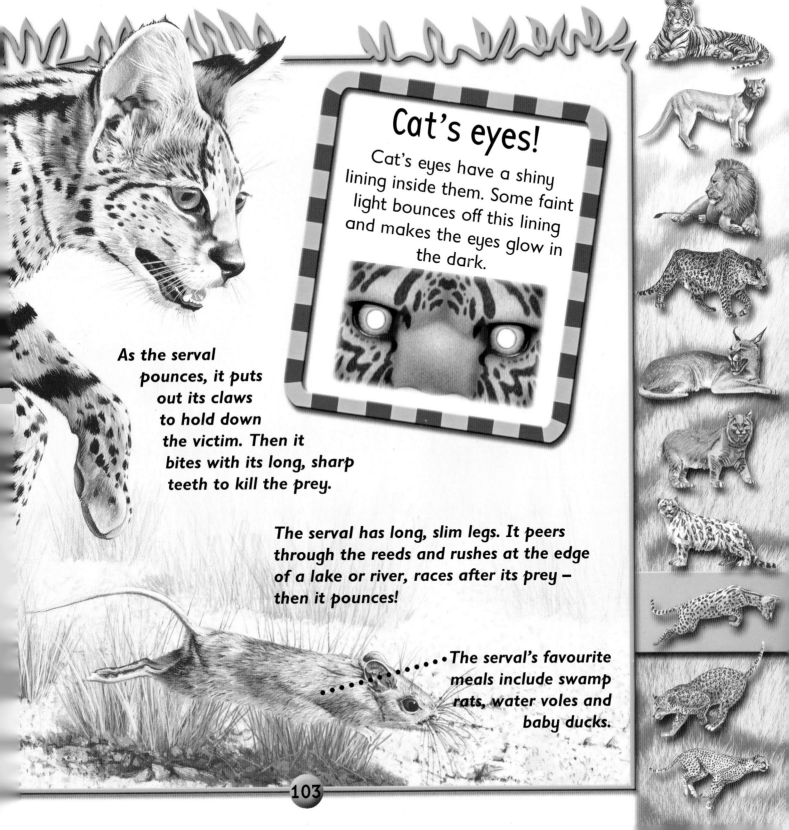

Cat's eyes!

Cat's eyes have a shiny lining inside them. Some faint light bounces off this lining and makes the eyes glow in the dark.

As the serval pounces, it puts out its claws to hold down the victim. Then it bites with its long, sharp teeth to kill the prey.

The serval has long, slim legs. It peers through the reeds and rushes at the edge of a lake or river, races after its prey – then it pounces!

The serval's favourite meals include swamp rats, water voles and baby ducks.

49 Leopards have a larder

Cat facts
• The leopard lives in many regions across Africa and southern Asia.
• It is about 2.5 metres in total length.

Sometimes a cat like the **LEOPARD** catches prey which is too big to eat in one meal. So the leopard stores the leftovers up in a tree. Here they are kept safe from hungry hyaenas and jackals too!

Leopards live in lots of places, from dry grassland and scrub to mountains, forests and swamps. They even live around villages.

The leopard may wait on a branch, and then pounce silently on a victim below.

Every leopard has a different pattern of spots – just like every person has different fingerprints.

Black leopard!

The black panther is not a different kind of big cat. It's a leopard with very dark fur.

The leopard's favourite tree has scratch marks in the bark. They warn other leopards to keep away.

The leopard is strong enough to drag a whole gazelle up into a tree.

A leopard can catch large animals such as antelopes, which are three times its own size. When food is scarce, it will eat rats, mice, birds' eggs, and even insects such as beetles!

50 The speedy cheetah

Cat facts

- The cheetah measures about 2 metres from nose to tail.

- It lives in Africa and western Asia.

No animal can run as fast as the **CHEETAH**. This big cat races along at 100 kilometres per hour – almost as fast as a car on a motorway. The cheetah can only keep up this speed for half a minute. Then it must stop to cool down and get its breath back.

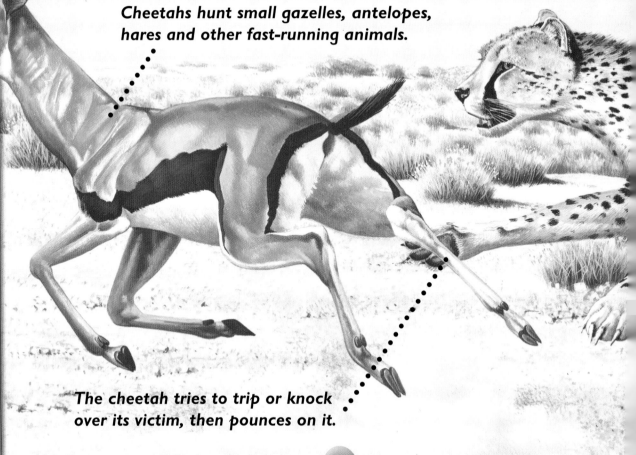

Cheetahs hunt small gazelles, antelopes, hares and other fast-running animals.

The cheetah tries to trip or knock over its victim, then pounces on it.

Cheetahs and many other kinds of big cat have become rare. Once, cats were killed for their fur, to make coats and hats. Today, all cats need our help to survive.

The cheetah likes dry, open places such as grassland and scrub. It cannot run very fast in a thick wood!

Claws out!

The cheetah is the only cat which cannot pull its claws into its toes. The claws are big and blunt, like a dog's.

The cheetah has a small head, a slim and bendy body, and very long legs.

Index

Acknowledgements

The publishers would like to thank the following
artists who have contributed to this book:

Sharks: John Butler
Dinosaurs: C.M. Buzer
Spiders: Richard Draper
Crocodiles: Steve Roberts
Big Cats: Ian Jackson